Discovering The World Around Us

RHINOS

Tough, Bad-Tempered and Dangerous

TJ Rob

RHINOS
Tough, Bad-Tempered and Dangerous
By TJ Rob

From the Discovering The World Around Us Series, Volume 3

Copyright Text TJ Rob, 2015

All rights reserved. No part of the book may be reproduced in any form without permission in writing from the author. Reviewers may quote brief passages in review.

ISBN 978-1-988695-12-9

Disclaimer:

No part of this book may be reproduced in any form or by any means, mechanical or electronic, including photocopying or recording, or by an information storage and retrieval system, or transmitted by email without permission in writing from the publisher. This book is for entertainment purposes only. The views expressed are those of author alone.

Published by:
TJ Rob
Suite 609
440-10816 Macleod Trail SE
Calgary, AB T2J 5N8 www.TJRob.com

Photo Credits: Images used under license from Fotolia.com and Shutterstock.com: Mike Lane /Fotolia.com pg. 1; jurra8 /Shutterstock.com pg. 4; Maxger /Shutterstock.com pg. 5; NY Studio /Shutterstock.com pg. 6; Derplan13 /Shutterstock.com pg. 7; Anna Rassadnikova /Shutterstock.com pg. 7; zoe field© /Fotolia.com pg. 8; zoe field /Fotolia.com pg. 9; Jiri Zuzanek; /Fotolia.com pg. 10; Bildagentur Zoonar GmbH /Shutterstock.com pg. 11; byrdyak /Fotolia.com pg. 12; Valdis Skudre /Shutterstock.com pg. 14; Valdis Skudre /Shutterstock.com pg. 15; Rob Francis /Shutterstock.com pg. 16; Maggy Meyer /Shutterstock.com pg. 16; fishcat007 /Fotolia.com pg. 17; smileimage9 /Shutterstock.com pg. 17; Palenque - Fotolia /Fotolia.com pg. 18; Palenque - Fotolia /Fotolia.com pg. 19; D J Noakes (Four Oaks) /Fotolia.com pg. 20; Michael Froehlich /Fotolia.com pg. 21; Linn Currie /Shutterstock.com pg. 22; JONATHAN PLEDGER /Shutterstock.com pg. 23; Stuart G Porter /Shutterstock.com pg. 24; Wongwiss /Shutterstock.com pg. 26; KsenyaLim /Shutterstock.com pg. 27; Tawin Mukdharakosa /Shutterstock.com pg. 27; john michael evan potter /Shutterstock.com pg. 28; Alta Oosthuizen /Shutterstock.com pg. 30; Alta Oosthuizen /Shutterstock.com pg. 31; Emi /Shutterstock.com pg. 32; Atthapol Saita /Shutterstock.com pg. 33; Vanatchanan /Shutterstock.com pg. 33; bazzlewazzle /Shutterstock.com pg. 34; Mari Swanepoel /Fotolia.com pg. 35; Mogens Trolle /Shutterstock.com pg. 36; LMspencer /Shutterstock.com pg. 37; Maggy Meyer /Shutterstock.com pg. 38; E.O. /Shutterstock.com pg. Back Cover; scooperdigital /Fotolia.com pg. Front Cover

TABLE OF CONTENTS	Page
What is a Rhino?	4
Where do Rhino live in the Wild today?	5
How big is a Rhino?	6
How many types of Rhino are there?	8
Africa's Black and White Rhinos	10
How long do Rhinos live?	14
What do Black Rhinos eat?	15
The Weird Mouth of the Black Rhino	16
What do White Rhinos eat?	17
How many babies do Rhinos have?	18
What are Rhinos horns made from?	22
What do Rhinos use their horns for?	23
Is a Rhino slow?	24
How thick is a Rhino's skin?	25
When does a Rhino sleep?	26
How well do Rhinos see, hear and smell?	27
Is the Rhino an aggressive and bad tempered animal?	29
Does a Rhino have enemies?	30
How bad is poaching?	32
How many Rhino are left in the wild?	33
Do Rhino fight each other?	34
How does a Rhino mark its territory?	36
How important is water?	37
A Rhino's best friend?	38
Some Rhino fun facts	39

What is a Rhino?

Rhinos are the 2nd largest land Mammals on Earth, after Elephants.

The full name for a Rhino is Rhinoceros.

We mostly use the shortened version of the name, Rhino.

The name Rhinoceros means "nose horn" in Greek.

It comes from the 2 Greek words "rhino" meaning nose and "ceros" meaning horn.

Where do Rhino live in the wild today?

The areas inside the red dotted lines are where we can find Rhino in the wild today

How Big is a Rhino?

Rhinos weigh up to 7,700 pounds (3500 kg).

A Rhino can stand up to 6 feet (1.8 meters) tall at the shoulders.

Rhinos grow to about 15 feet (4.6 meters) long.

A Rhino is as tall as a man and as heavy as 2 cars.

How many types of Rhino are there?

There are 5 types or species of Rhino altogether – 3 in Asia and 2 in Africa.

The 2 African Rhinos are the Black and White Rhino.

The other 3 types – Indian, Sumatran and Javan are all found in Asia.

The African Rhinos are more well-known, and that is why we will be looking at them in greater detail in this book.

Africa's Black and White Rhinos

Both Black and White Rhino are actually grey in color.

The Black Rhino has almost a beak shaped mouth while the White Rhino has a wider mouth and lips.

The Black Rhino is also called the Hook-lipped Rhino.

Black Rhino
Rounder, beak shaped mouth

Black and White Rhinos

White Rhinos are bigger than Black Rhinos.

The early Dutch settlers used the Dutch word for wide "wyd".

The name became misinterpreted for the English word "white".

So even though it is not white, the name stuck, and we use the name White Rhino today.

98.8% of White Rhinos and 96.1% of Black Rhinos are found in just four countries:

South Africa, Namibia, Zimbabwe and Kenya.

How long do Rhinos live?

In the wild, Black Rhinos live for 30 to 35 years.

White Rhinos live up to 45 years.

Other species of Rhinos live for 30 to 40 years.

Rhinos live a few years longer in captivity than they do in the wild.

What do Black Rhinos eat?

Black Rhinos prefer woodlands with thorn tree thickets.

The thick bush serves as cover and provides Black Rhinos with their favorite food of small trees, bushes, twigs and leaves.

A Black Rhino is mainly a browser but will occasionally eat some grass and herbs.

The Weird Mouth of a Black Rhino

A Black Rhino pulls buds, leaves and twigs into its mouth with its triangular shaped upper lip.

They also eat fruit.

Its upper lip can bend in all directions, just like a Giraffe's tongue.

What do White Rhinos eat?

White Rhinos are the only grazers among the five Rhino species, feeding almost only on short grasses.

They live mainly in grassy savanna areas and in woodlands with lots of grassy clearings.

How many babies do Rhinos have?

The Rhino has the second longest pregnancy in the world, after Elephants.

Rhino pregnancy is long at between 15 to 16 months.

Normally Rhinos only have 1 calf that weighs about 100 pounds (45 kg) at birth.

Calves can walk 10 minutes after they are born.

The mother will keep it hidden for a couple of weeks in fear that it may get trampled upon.

Females are also called cows. They have 1 calf every 2 to 5 years.

Rhino calves are preyed upon by Lions and Spotted Hyenas.

A Rhino cow is always very quick to defend her calf against actual and potential danger.

Cows with calves are especially dangerous and will charge any time they feel threatened.

Although they nurse for a year, calves are able to begin eating vegetation a few weeks after birth.

A Rhino calf stays with its mother until it is about 2 to 4 years old, when she has her next calf.

The mother pushes away an older calf that stays around after the birth of a new calf.

What are Rhino horns made from?

All African Rhinos (the Black and White Rhino) have 2 horns.

One large horn is found at the tip of its nose and one shorter horn higher up on its nose, almost between its eyes.

Two of the Asian Rhinos, the Indian Rhino and the Javan Rhino, have only one horn. The last Asian species, the Sumatran Rhino, has two horns.

It was once thought that Rhino horn was made up of compressed hair.

Today we know that the horn is made of keratin - the same material that nails, claws and hooves are made of.

What do Rhinos use their horns for?

They use their horns to defend their territories and to defend calves from other Rhinos and predators.

Rhino mothers use their horns to nudge and guide calves.

Rhinos also use their horns to dig for water and to break branches.

The longest measured horn was 4 feet and 9 inches (1.45 meters) long.

A Rhino horn might weigh up to 11 pounds (5 Kilograms).

Is a Rhino slow?

No, Rhino are very fast runners.

For short distances they can run as fast as a horse, reaching speeds of 40 miles per hour (60 kilometers per hour).

They are also able to turn sharply in a small space.

How thick is a Rhino's skin?

Rhinos usually have gray skin, although their individual shade depends on the soil conditions where they live and graze.

The skin on certain parts of their bodies, especially their shoulders, can be as much as 1.5 inches (3.4 centimeters) thick.

Their skin is wrinkled with almost no hair.

Even though Rhino skin is extremely thick, Rhinos cannot sweat.

Similar to an Elephant, a Rhino will roll in mud or dust to keep it cool. The mud also gives it a protective coating against biting insects.

This is Rhino skin!

When does a Rhino sleep?

Rhinos need to sleep for about 8 or 9 hours each day.

They will usually sleep in stages throughout the day.

During very hot periods, they cool off by bathing in mud in shallow pools.

Rhinos sleep deeply and can even be approached without them knowing while they are asleep.

They are usually active in the early morning and late afternoon and very active at night when it is cooler.

How well do Rhinos see, hear and smell?

Rhinos have really poor eyesight.

Their eyesight is so bad that sometimes they attack trees and rocks that are only a few feet (meters) away, mistaking them for other animals.

Rhinos do have a great sense of smell and great hearing that makes up for their bad eyesight.

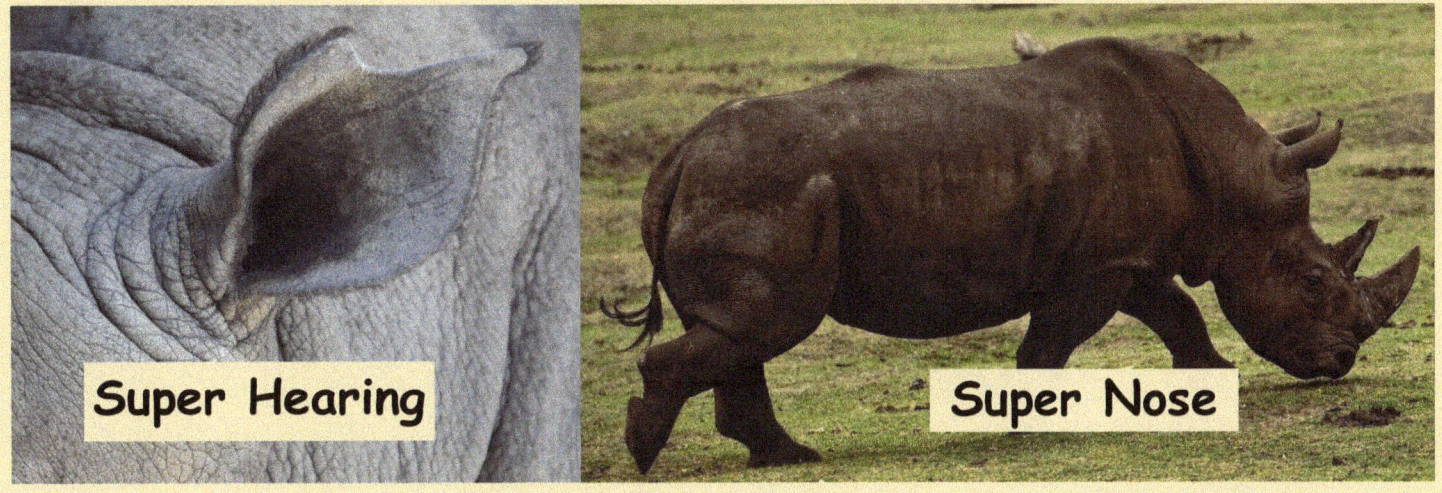

Super Hearing

Super Nose

When there is wind in their favor they can probably smell a human from at least 600 feet (200 meters) away.

That's more than the length of 2 football fields.

Don't mess with a charging Black Rhino!

Is the Rhino an aggressive and bad tempered animal?

The Black Rhino does indeed have a reputation for having a bad temper.

Black Rhinos are considered to be more unpredictable and excitable than White Rhinos.

Black Rhinos can be very aggressive and can react by attacking the threat, even a poacher.

They have even been known to wait in thick bushes and ambush people.

White Rhino are more sociable and calmer than Black Rhino.

White Rhinos respond to threats by running away to a safe distance.

Does a Rhino have enemies?

Rhino calves are at risk from being attacked, but adult Rhinos have no natural enemies in the wild.

Man is their deadliest enemy. Rhinos are now among the most endangered species on Earth, because of hunting and poaching.

Hunters are attracted to the Rhino's magnificent horn, which is valued for ornaments and medicine.

Bits of crushed horn are a prized ingredient in some Asian medicines.

Some Rhinos have been de-horned to make them worthless to poachers!

How bad is poaching?

Poaching has devastated Rhino populations, and the number is getting smaller every day.

150 years ago there were 1,000,000 African Rhinos (Black and White Rhinos).

Today there are less than 5,000 Black Rhino and 20,000 White Rhino still left in the wild.

There are less than 50 Javan Rhino that survive today. The only Javan Rhino are to be found in Indonesia's Ujung Kulon National Park. None exist in zoos.

The Black Rhino, Javan Rhino and Sumatran Rhino are all Critically Endangered.

This means they have a very good chance of becoming totally extinct in the next 75 years.

How many Rhino are left in the wild?

Estimated Rhino in the Wild Today:

White Rhino	20,000
Black Rhino	5,000
Indian Rhino	3,500
Sumatran Rhino	Less than 200
Javan Rhino	Less than 50

Do Rhino fight each other?

Fights between wild Rhino are rare because they mostly avoid each other.

Fights can occur when two males are courting the same female. Male Rhinos are called bulls.

Some disputes are settled without physical combat.

This happens when one male leaves after a no nonsense stare from the other bull or when there is a charge from one of the bulls.

If two bulls do fight they fight with sideways blows of their heads and horns.

Fights can become vicious and battle wounds are the main cause of death among 8 to 10 year-old young bulls.

Black Rhinos have the highest rate of death among mammals in fights among the same species.

How does a Rhino mark its territory?

Rhinos use piles of dung to leave "messages" for other Rhinos.

Each Rhino's smell is unique and identifies its owner.

It can also tell a Rhino if the other Rhino is young, old, male or female.

They also tell other Rhinos that this is their territory.

How important is water?

Since it needs to drink at least once a day, Rhinos stay within 3 miles (5 km) of water.

White Rhinos drink up to 20 gallons (75 liters) per day. Black Rhinos drink a bit less per day.

If they have to, Rhinos can survive for 4 or 5 days without water by eating grasses and plants that have moisture in their leaves.

In very dry conditions, Rhinos will dig for water using their front feet.

A Rhino's best friend?

The Oxpecker bird eats ticks and other insects that it finds on the Rhino, and makes a noise when it senses danger.

This helps alert the Rhino.

Some Rhino Fun Facts

1. A group of Rhinos is called a crash.

2. All Rhinos have 3 toes on each foot.

3. Rhinos closest relatives are Zebras, Horses and Tapirs all known as odd-toed ungulates (three toes on each foot).

4. Rhinos haven't changed much since prehistoric times (though of course they were a lot woollier back then!).

5. Some of the first Rhinos didn't have horns and once roamed throughout North America and Europe.

6. No Rhino species have ever inhabited South America, Australia or New Zealand.

THANKS FOR READING!

Please leave a review at the website where you bought this book and tell others what you liked about it.

Visit www.TJRob.com for a FREE eBook and to see TJ Rob's other exciting books

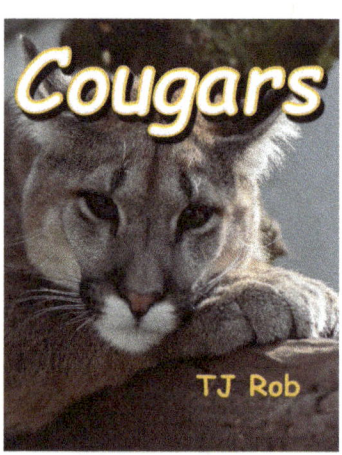

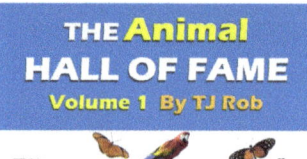

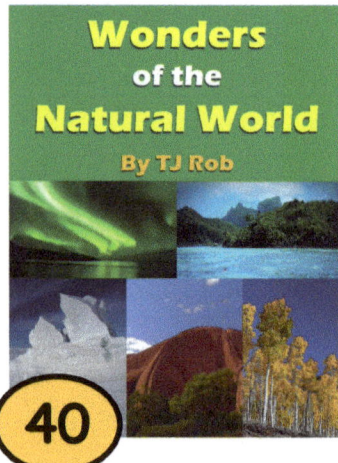
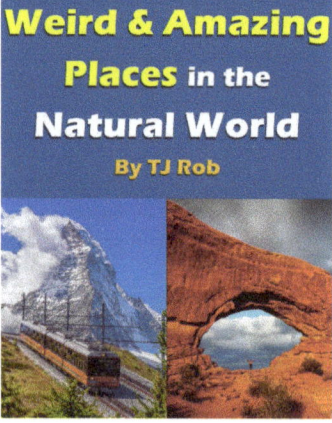

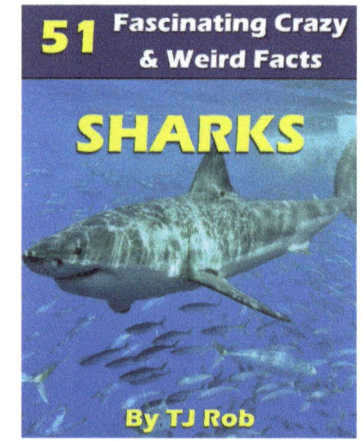

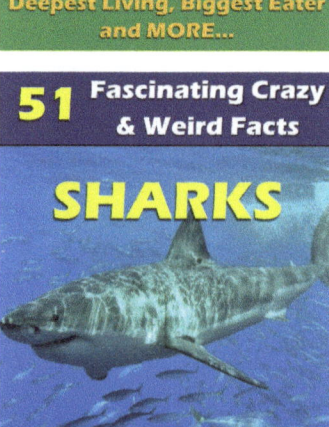

www.ingramcontent.com/pod-product-compliance
Lightning Source LLC
Chambersburg PA
CBHW040005080526
44586CB00027B/2888